Teacher Journal
Daily Reflection

Date: Mo Tu
We Thu Fr

Word of the day:

_____

Challenges of the day:

Wins of the day:

Notes:

_____
_____
_____
_____
_____
_____
_____
_____
_____

To-do list:

Top priorities:

Best part of today:

Worst part of today:

Mood during the day

Bad

○ ○ ○ ○ ○ ○

Perfect

Date: Mo Tu
We Thu Fr
Word of the day:

_____

Challenges of the day:

Wins of the day:

Notes:

_____
_____
_____
_____
_____
_____
_____
_____
_____

To-do list:

Top priorities:

Best part of today:

Worst part of today:

Mood during the day

Bad

○   ○   ○   ○   ○   ○

Perfect

Date: Mo   Tu
We   Thu   Fr

Word of the day:

_____

Challenges of the day:

Wins of the day:

Notes:

_____
_____
_____
_____
_____
_____
_____
_____
_____

To-do list:

Top priorities:

Best part of today:

Worst part of today:

Mood during the day

Bad

O   O   O   O   O   O

Perfect

Date: Mo   Tu

We   Thu   Fr

Word of the day:

Challenges of the day:

Wins of the day:

Notes:

_____

_____

_____

_____

_____

_____

_____

_____

_____

To-do list:

Top priorities:

Best part of today:

Worst part of today:

Mood during the day

Bad

O   O   O   O   O   O

Perfect

Date: Mo Tu
We Thu Fr

Word of the day:

Challenges of the day:

Wins of the day:

Notes:

To-do list:

Top priorities:

Best part of today:

Worst part of today:

Mood during the day

Bad

○   ○   ○   ○   ○   ○

Perfect

Date: Mo Tu

We Thu Fr

Word of the day:

Challenges of the day:

Wins of the day:

Notes:

To-do list:

Top priorities:

Best part of today:

Worst part of today:

Bad

Mood during the day

○　　　○　　　○　　　○　　　○　　　○

Perfect

Date: Mo Tu
We Thu Fr

Word of the day:

_____

Challenges of the day:

Wins of the day:

Notes:

_____
_____
_____
_____
_____
_____
_____
_____
_____

To-do list:

Top priorities:

Best part of today:

Worst part of today:

Bad

Mood during the day

O   O   O   O   O   O

Perfect

Date: Mo Tu
We Thu Fr

Word of the day:

Challenges of the day:

Wins of the day:

Notes:
_____
_____
_____
_____
_____
_____
_____
_____
_____

To-do list:

Top priorities:

Best part of today:

Worst part of today:

Mood during the day

Bad

O   O   O   O   O   O

Perfect

Date: Mo Tu
We Thu Fr

Word of the day:

Challenges of the day:

Wins of the day:

Notes:

_____
_____
_____
_____
_____
_____
_____
_____
_____

To-do list:

Top priorities:

Best part of today:

Worst part of today:

Bad

Mood during the day

○   ○   ○   ○   ○   ○

Perfect

Date: Mo   Tu
We   Thu   Fr

Word of the day:

Challenges of the day:

Wins of the day:

Notes:

_____

_____

_____

_____

_____

_____

_____

_____

_____

To-do list:

Top priorities:

Best part of today:

Worst part of today:

Bad

Mood during the day

○   ○   ○   ○   ○   ○

Perfect

Date: Mo Tu
We Thu Fr

Word of the day:

Challenges of the day:

Wins of the day:

Notes:

_____

_____

_____

_____

_____

_____

_____

_____

To-do list:

Top priorities:

Best part of today:

Worst part of today:

Mood during the day

Bad

○   ○   ○   ○   ○   ○

Perfect

Date: Mo Tu
We Thu Fr
Word of the day:

Challenges of the day:

Wins of the day:

Notes:
_____
_____
_____
_____
_____
_____
_____
_____
_____

To-do list:

Top priorities:

Best part of today:

Worst part of today:

Bad

Mood during the day

○　　　○　　　○　　　○　　　○　　　○

Perfect

Date: Mo Tu
We Thu Fr

Word of the day:

Challenges of the day:

Wins of the day:

Notes:

_____

_____

_____

_____

_____

_____

_____

_____

_____

To-do list:

Top priorities:

Best part of today:

Worst part of today:

Mood during the day

Bad

O   O   O   O   O   O

Perfect

Date: Mo   Tu

We   Thu   Fr

Word of the day:

Challenges of the day:

Wins of the day:

Notes:

_____

_____

_____

_____

_____

_____

_____

_____

_____

To-do list:

Top priorities:

Best part of today:

Worst part of today:

Mood during the day

Bad

O   O   O   O   O   O

Perfect

Date: Mo Tu
We Thu Fr

Word of the day:

_____

Challenges of the day:

Wins of the day:

Notes:

_____

_____

_____

_____

_____

_____

_____

_____

_____

To-do list:

Top priorities:

Best part of today:

Worst part of today:

Mood during the day

Bad

O   O   O   O   O   O

Perfect

Date: Mo Tu
We Thu Fr

Word of the day:

Challenges of the day:

Wins of the day:

Notes:

_____
_____
_____
_____
_____
_____
_____
_____
_____

To-do list:

Top priorities:

Best part of today:

Worst part of today:

Bad

Mood during the day

○   ○   ○   ○   ○   ○

Perfect

Date: Mo Tu
We Thu Fr
Word of the day:

Challenges of the day:

Wins of the day:

Notes:
_____
_____
_____
_____
_____
_____
_____
_____
_____

To-do list:

Top priorities:

Best part of today:

Worst part of today:

Mood during the day

Bad

Perfect

Date: Mo   Tu

We   Thu   Fr

Word of the day:

Challenges of the day:

Wins of the day:

Notes:

_____

_____

_____

_____

_____

_____

_____

_____

_____

To-do list:

Top priorities:

Best part of today:

Worst part of today:

Bad

Mood during the day

O   O   O   O   O   O

Perfect

Date: Mo Tu
We Thu Fr

Word of the day:

Challenges of the day:

Wins of the day:

Notes:

To-do list:

Top priorities:

Best part of today:

Worst part of today:

Mood during the day

Bad

O   O   O   O   O   O

Perfect

Date: Mo Tu
We Thu Fr
Word of the day:

Challenges of the day:

Wins of the day:

Notes:
_____
_____
_____
_____
_____
_____
_____
_____
_____

To-do list:

Top priorities:

Best part of today:

Worst part of today:

Mood during the day

Bad

○　　　○　　　○　　　○　　　○　　　○

Perfect

Date: Mo   Tu

We   Thu   Fr

Word of the day:

Challenges of the day:

Wins of the day:

Notes:

_____

_____

_____

_____

_____

_____

_____

_____

_____

To-do list:

Top priorities:

Best part of today:

Worst part of today:

Mood during the day

Bad

O   O   O   O   O   O

Perfect

Date: Mo Tu

We Thu Fr

Word of the day:

Challenges of the day:

Wins of the day:

Notes:

_____

_____

_____

_____

_____

_____

_____

_____

To-do list:

Top priorities:

Best part of today:

Worst part of today:

Bad

Mood during the day

○   ○   ○   ○   ○   ○

Perfect

Date: Mo Tu
We Thu Fr
Word of the day:

Challenges of the day:

Wins of the day:

Notes:
_____
_____
_____
_____
_____
_____
_____
_____
_____

To-do list:

Top priorities:

Best part of today:

Worst part of today:

Mood during the day

Bad

○ ○ ○ ○ ○ ○

Perfect

Date: Mo   Tu
We   Thu   Fr

Word of the day:

Challenges of the day:

Wins of the day:

Notes:

_____
_____
_____
_____
_____
_____
_____
_____
_____

To-do list:

Top priorities:

Best part of today:

Worst part of today:

Bad

Mood during the day

O   O   O   O   O   O

Perfect

Date: Mo Tu

We Thu Fr

Word of the day:

Challenges of the day:

Wins of the day:

Notes:

_____
_____
_____
_____
_____
_____
_____
_____
_____

To-do list:

Top priorities:

Best part of today:

Worst part of today:

Bad

Mood during the day

O   O   O   O   O   O

Perfect

Date: Mo Tu
We Thu Fr

Word of the day:

Challenges of the day:

Wins of the day:

Notes:

_____
_____
_____
_____
_____
_____
_____
_____
_____

To-do list:

Top priorities:

Best part of today:

Worst part of today:

Mood during the day

Bad

○   ○   ○   ○   ○   ○

Perfect

Date: Mo   Tu
We   Thu   Fr
Word of the day:

Challenges of the day:

Wins of the day:

Notes:
_____
_____
_____
_____
_____
_____
_____
_____
_____

To-do list:

Top priorities:

Best part of today:

Worst part of today:

Bad

Mood during the day

O   O   O   O   O   O

Perfect

Date: Mo Tu
We Thu Fr
Word of the day:

Challenges of the day:

Wins of the day:

Notes:

_____
_____
_____
_____
_____
_____
_____
_____
_____

To-do list:

Top priorities:

Best part of today:

Worst part of today:

Bad

Mood during the day

○   ○   ○   ○   ○   ○

Perfect

Date: Mo   Tu
We   Thu   Fr

Word of the day:

Challenges of the day:

Wins of the day:

Notes:

_____

_____

_____

_____

_____

_____

_____

_____

To-do list:

Top priorities:

Best part of today:

Worst part of today:

Mood during the day

Bad

○   ○   ○   ○   ○   ○

Perfect

Date: Mo Tu
We Thu Fr

Word of the day:

_____

Challenges of the day:

Wins of the day:

Notes:

_____

_____

_____

_____

_____

_____

_____

_____

To-do list:

Top priorities:

Best part of today:

Worst part of today:

Mood during the day

Bad

○   ○   ○   ○   ○   ○

Perfect

Date: Mo   Tu
We   Thu   Fr

Word of the day:

Challenges of the day:

Wins of the day:

Notes:

_____

_____

_____

_____

_____

_____

_____

_____

_____

To-do list:

Top priorities:

Best part of today:

Worst part of today:

Bad

Mood during the day

○　　　○　　　○　　　○　　　○　　　○

Perfect

Date: Mo Tu
We Thu Fr

Word of the day:

Challenges of the day:

Wins of the day:

Notes:

_____
_____
_____
_____
_____
_____
_____
_____
_____

To-do list:

Top priorities:

Best part of today:

Worst part of today:

Mood during the day

Bad

○　　　　○　　　　○　　　　○　　　　○　　　　○

Perfect

Date: Mo   Tu
We   Thu   Fr

Word of the day:

Challenges of the day:

Wins of the day:

Notes:

_____
_____
_____
_____
_____
_____
_____
_____
_____

To-do list:

Top priorities:

Best part of today:

Worst part of today:

Bad

Mood during the day

○   ○   ○   ○   ○   ○

Perfect

Date: Mo   Tu
We   Thu   Fr

Word of the day:

Challenges of the day:

Wins of the day:

Notes:

_____

_____

_____

_____

_____

_____

_____

_____

_____

To-do list:

Top priorities:

Best part of today:

Worst part of today:

Bad

Mood during the day

O   O   O   O   O   O

Perfect

Date: Mo   Tu
We   Thu   Fr

Word of the day:

Challenges of the day:

Wins of the day:

Notes:

_____

_____

_____

_____

_____

_____

_____

_____

To-do list:

Top priorities:

Best part of today:

Worst part of today:

Mood during the day

Bad

○   ○   ○   ○   ○   ○

Perfect

Date: Mo   Tu
We   Thu   Fr

Word of the day:

Challenges of the day:

Wins of the day:

Notes:

_____

_____

_____

_____

_____

_____

_____

_____

_____

To-do list:

Top priorities:

Best part of today:

Worst part of today:

Mood during the day

Bad

O   O   O   O   O   O

Perfect

Date: Mo Tu
We Thu Fr

Word of the day:

Challenges of the day:

Wins of the day:

Notes:

_____
_____
_____
_____
_____
_____
_____
_____
_____

To-do list:

Top priorities:

Best part of today:

Worst part of today:

Bad

Mood during the day

O   O   O   O   O   O

Perfect

Date: Mo Tu
We Thu Fr
Word of the day:

Challenges of the day:

Wins of the day:

Notes:

_____
_____
_____
_____
_____
_____
_____
_____
_____

To-do list:

Top priorities:

Best part of today:

Worst part of today:

Mood during the day

Bad

Perfect

O   O   O   O   O   O

Date: Mo   Tu
We   Thu   Fr

Word of the day:

Challenges of the day:

Wins of the day:

Notes:

_____

_____

_____

_____

_____

_____

_____

_____

_____

To-do list:

Top priorities:

Best part of today:

Worst part of today:

Mood during the day

Bad

O   O   O   O   O   O

Perfect

Date: Mo Tu
We Thu Fr

Word of the day:

Challenges of the day:

Wins of the day:

Notes:

_____
_____
_____
_____
_____
_____
_____
_____
_____

To-do list:

Top priorities:

Best part of today:

Worst part of today:

Bad

Mood during the day

O   O   O   O   O   O

Perfect

Date: Mo   Tu
We   Thu   Fr

Word of the day:

Challenges of the day:

Wins of the day:

Notes:

_____
_____
_____
_____
_____
_____
_____
_____
_____

To-do list:

Top priorities:

Best part of today:

Worst part of today:

Bad

Mood during the day

O   O   O   O   O   O

Perfect

Date: Mo Tu
We Thu Fr

Word of the day:

Challenges of the day:

Wins of the day:

Notes:

To-do list:

Top priorities:

Best part of today:

Worst part of today:

Bad

Mood during the day

O   O   O   O   O   O

Perfect

Date: Mo Tu
We Thu Fr
Word of the day:

Challenges of the day:

Wins of the day:

Notes:

_____

_____

_____

_____

_____

_____

_____

_____

_____

To-do list:

Top priorities:

Best part of today:

Worst part of today:

Bad

Mood during the day

○   ○   ○   ○   ○   ○

Perfect

Date: Mo   Tu
We   Thu   Fr

Word of the day:

Challenges of the day:

Wins of the day:

Notes:

_____
_____
_____
_____
_____
_____
_____
_____
_____

To-do list:

Top priorities:

Best part of today:

Worst part of today:

Mood during the day

Bad

○   ○   ○   ○   ○   ○

Perfect

Date: Mo Tu
We Thu Fr

Word of the day:

Challenges of the day:

Wins of the day:

Notes:

_____
_____
_____
_____
_____
_____
_____
_____
_____

To-do list:

Top priorities:

Best part of today:

Worst part of today:

Bad

Mood during the day

O   O   O   O   O   O

Perfect

Date: Mo Tu
We Thu Fr
Word of the day:

Challenges of the day:

Wins of the day:

Notes:

_____
_____
_____
_____
_____
_____
_____
_____
_____

To-do list:

Top priorities:

Best part of today:

Worst part of today:

Bad

Mood during the day

O   O   O   O   O   O

Perfect

Date: Mo Tu
We Thu Fr
Word of the day:
_____

Challenges of the day:

Wins of the day:

Notes:
_____
_____
_____
_____
_____
_____
_____
_____
_____

To-do list:

Top priorities:

Best part of today:

Worst part of today:

Mood during the day

Bad

O   O   O   O   O   O

Perfect

Date: Mo Tu
We Thu Fr

Word of the day:

Challenges of the day:

Wins of the day:

Notes:

_____
_____
_____
_____
_____
_____
_____
_____
_____

To-do list:

Top priorities:

Best part of today:

Worst part of today:

Mood during the day

Bad

O   O   O   O   O   O

Perfect

Date: Mo Tu
We Thu Fr
Word of the day:

Challenges of the day:

Wins of the day:

Notes:

_____
_____
_____
_____
_____
_____
_____
_____
_____

To-do list:

Top priorities:

Best part of today:

Worst part of today:

Mood during the day

Bad

O   O   O   O   O   O

Perfect

Date: Mo Tu
We Thu Fr

Word of the day:

_____

Challenges of the day:

Wins of the day:

Notes:

_____
_____
_____
_____
_____
_____
_____
_____
_____

To-do list:

Top priorities:

Best part of today:

Worst part of today:

Mood during the day

Bad

O   O   O   O   O   O

Perfect

Date: Mo   Tu
We   Thu   Fr

Word of the day:

_____

Challenges of the day:

Wins of the day:

Notes:

_____
_____
_____
_____
_____
_____
_____
_____
_____

To-do list:

Top priorities:

Best part of today:

Worst part of today:

Bad

Mood during the day

○   ○   ○   ○   ○   ○

Perfect

Date: Mo Tu

We Thu Fr

Word of the day:

Challenges of the day:

Wins of the day:

Notes:

To-do list:

Top priorities:

Best part of today:

Worst part of today:

Mood during the day

Bad

O   O   O   O   O   O

Perfect

Date: Mo   Tu
We   Thu   Fr

Word of the day:

Challenges of the day:

Wins of the day:

Notes:

_____
_____
_____
_____
_____
_____
_____
_____
_____

To-do list:

Top priorities:

Best part of today:

Worst part of today:

Bad

Mood during the day

O   O   O   O   O   O

Perfect

Date: Mo Tu
We Thu Fr

Word of the day:

_____

Challenges of the day:

Wins of the day:

Notes:

_____

_____

_____

_____

_____

_____

_____

_____

_____

To-do list:

Top priorities:

Best part of today:

Worst part of today:

Mood during the day

Bad

○   ○   ○   ○   ○   ○

Perfect

Date: Mo Tu
We Thu Fr
Word of the day:

Challenges of the day:

Wins of the day:

Notes:

_____
_____
_____
_____
_____
_____
_____
_____
_____

To-do list:

Top priorities:

Best part of today:

Worst part of today:

Bad

Mood during the day

○   ○   ○   ○   ○   ○

Perfect

Made in United States
Troutdale, OR
04/20/2024

19327201R00066